Sports Entrepreneur

A Guide to Bring Your Sports Product or Service Business Idea to Life

David Smith

B180 Basketball, Inc
P.O. Box 2406
Midland, MI 48641-2406
www.b180basketball.com
Phone: 1-800-957-1275

© 2017 by David Smith. All rights reserved.

No part of this book may be reproduced, stored in a retrieval system, or transmitted by any means without written permission of the author.

Published by B180 Basketball, Inc. 11/17/2017

ISBN: 978-0-692-97259-5 (sc)
ISBN: 978-0-692-97258-8 (e)

Library of Congress Control Number: 2017916937

Any persons depicted in stock imagery are models and such images are being used for illustrative purposes only.

Because of the dynamic nature of the Internet, any web addresses or links contained in this book may have changed since publication and may no longer be valid. The views expressed in this work are solely those of the author and do not necessarily reflect the views of the publisher, and the publisher hereby disclaims any responsibility for them.

Contents

DEDICATION v
ACKNOWLEDGMENTS..i
Introduction 1
Five Guidelines for Sports Entrepreneurs 3
Creating a Product from an Idea................................13
Creating a Service Business from an Idea 18
Protecting Your Product or Service Business Idea 25
Finding Someone to Design Your Product 30
Designing Your Packaging Box 34
Finding Supplies for Your Service Business 38
Building Your Team..42
Writing a Business Plan 48
Seek Business Assistance..53
Finding Money to Fund Your Business 57

DEDICATION

This book is dedicated to my mother, Connie Smith. Thank you for always believing in me and listening to me. You loved me unconditionally, taught me the value of caring & giving, and how to be a friend. I'm thankful that you and dad were married for over 30 years. I learn so much from you and cherish every moment I'm around you. I love you.

ACKNOWLEDGMENTS

I'd like to acknowledge all the coaches, student athletes, professional athletes, and sports enthusiast that have a passion for entrepreneurship and sports. Your drive, commitment and desire for sports have developed and put in your mind ideas, dreams, and talents that only you can bring to life.

Introduction

The sports business industry is very broad and full of opportunities for entrepreneurs. Whether it's creating a new sports product or opening a fitness training business, the chance to be your own boss and thrive in a competitive and passion-driven industry is growing. Sport management students, sports enthusiast, and people from all walks of life have the ideas, passion, drive, and commitment to increase the emergence of new and unique businesses within the sports industry. The sport enthusiast or athlete may have an idea for making a sport better. They may have an idea for an entirely new type of sport. Where do they start? What should they do first? Who should they tell about their idea? This book is designed to walk you step by step through the process of bringing your idea to life, protecting it, and getting help to fund expansion. Many topics will be discussed to prepare and guide you through the development process before seeking outside assistance.

Read each chapter with an open, creative, and outside of the box thought process. Refer to the chapter that closely matches the stage you are in as you attempt to bring your product or service business to life. Write down business ideas as you read along. Highlight, underline, and circle comments or sections that stand out to you.

Note:

The views in this book are the authors'. For additional information on starting a business, you can find resources in your local community.

Five Guidelines for Sports Entrepreneurs

- Create and Protect
- Stay Motivated Daily
- Educate Yourself
- Build a Team
- Be Persistent

Create and Protect

Creating a sports product or service business takes passion for what you are doing. If you don't love it wholeheartedly and are not willing to sacrifice almost anything for it, then it's the wrong product or service business. You have to be committed when times are rough, and nobody understands, cares, or knows about your product or service. As you brainstorm idea after idea, one idea will have you always thinking about it. This is the one to go with. When you decide to go forward with what you've been thinking about by drawing a sketch of it, an idea is finally acted upon and created. Procedures and tasks must be in place to protect your idea from being copied or your concept stolen before you bring it fully to life. That is, before you are fully able to share and market it to the world. A decision has to be made on how to best protect your idea. Will it be a copyright or trademark protection? Will you seek patent protection? What type of company should be formed to fit your product or service business best? These questions must be answered. In other words, you will need help when bringing your idea to life. That doesn't mean that you have to give up a large portion of ownership in your newly formed business to do so.

There is another way to bring your idea to life without giving up a large portion of your company. That way is for entrepreneurs to keep full control of their company; bring their ideas and concepts to life with no problems at all and have success. Entrepreneurs that choose not to follow the objective of keeping control of their company may be met with consequences. They may give up and quit altogether because they are not sure of what to do next. Then there are others that simply lose control of their company, have their idea stolen, or they may take a buyout. That is, they will sell their idea without fully seeing how large their business can actually grow by keeping it.

Protecting your idea is similar to protecting and caring for a newborn baby. Being very careful and paying attention to detail about every aspect of your business is key. The time is right to tell someone about your idea is when it's fully protected. Filling out an application and registering a copyright, trademark, or patent must be done before moving forward. Hire a lawyer or another professional to assist you with the filling out and registering of the application. If you choose to do it alone, be careful to make sure that everything on the application is filled out correctly. Make sure that all of your signatures are in the correct places on the application. Finally, make sure that you pay the fee that is required to properly register your copyright, trademark, or patent.

As a young entrepreneur, I had an idea about a fitness business. The idea came from when I visited a fitness center in a different state. I observed the entire layout of the building. I then thought to myself, this type of fitness center would be beneficial in my hometown. I had additional concepts and ideas that I wanted to add to the fitness business that was to be operating in my hometown. I didn't know where to start. So, I decided to write a business plan first. After writing the business plan I went to a local agency to seek assistance and share my ideas and plan. The individual that I talked to at the agency seemed confused and uncertain about my plan because it was new and different from other fitness businesses in the community. After meeting with the agency I was unsure of what to do next. I eventually just let the business plan sit and collect dust on a shelf in my home. During the time that I met with the agency, I did not have the person that I met with sign a non-disclosure agreement. I didn't even apply for a copyright, trademark, or patent on anything that could be protected.

About three years later, a fitness business opened in my hometown. To my amazement, most of the concepts and ideas that I had presented to the agency were features that the new fitness business had. I learned a valuable lesson because of this experience. Now I'm sharing it with you with the hope that you remember to create an idea, then protect it before sharing. Also, when met with uncertainty or confusion, seek assistance carefully and continue to move forward day by day and bring your idea to life.

Stay Motivated Daily

You have to have a daily vision of your end product or service. The vision that you have should be of your idea or concept being complete and is helping the world. Motivating yourself daily to do this has to be done. It takes discipline and a willingness to seek out a variety of strategies to motivate yourself. One day it may be listening to music. Another day it may be a motivational speaker. Whatever you choose to do daily to motivate yourself, make sure that it starts with writing down a single goal that will bring your idea closer to existence if you complete it on that particular day. Remember, you will have daily life events and many people telling you things that will bring your confidence and overall spirit down. Stay positive. Think positive. Read quotes. Attend events and social gatherings that connect you with other positive and successful people. Daily motivational strategies help stimulate your mind to come up with new ways to improve your idea or concept. When that new idea or concept enters your mind, quickly write it down.

Watching movies is another way to stay motivated. As an entrepreneur, I enjoy and am always inspired after watching short workout or fitness training monologues from movies. My favorite movies to watch are the Rocky movie series. I also listen to various motivational speakers, read success quotes daily, exercise weekly, and read my own personal goals list daily. Something that has always motivated me are my parents. When I think of them and all of the good things they have done for my siblings and myself, it pushes me to another level and encourages me to want to make them proud of me. I sometimes look at family pictures or study other successful businesses to get me motivated as well. Doing these things not only gets me motivated, but it also helps me to generate new strategies and concepts to improve the ideas that I create or have already created.

Whatever strategies you choose to motivate yourself daily, always remember to end your day by reading your list of personal goals for your life. Read them at night before you go to bed. That way it's what you think about when you are sleeping.

Educate Yourself

In order to bring your idea to life, you have to become a lifelong learner. Educate yourself thoroughly in your chosen field of expertise. Also, be keen and insightful in multiple areas within business, sport, and the world. This will help broaden your understanding of the world. It will also play a role in shaping your ideas and determine how it will help better the world by its existence. There are many strategies and ways to learn on your own and at your own pace. Decide to attend a seminar or another event that interests you and is in your area of expertise. Reading books, talking to experts or mentors in your field of interest, watching inspiring videos, listening to recordings about successful entrepreneurs, being around other successful individuals and studying their behaviors and ways of doing things are all effective strategies to educate yourself. If you decide that reading is an option that you'd like to explore, try to read at least one book a month.

Continuously educating yourself keeps you current and aware of new trends and concepts in your field or area of expertise. It also challenges you daily to apply what you've learned. You will be able to create a unique and new product or service based on something that you learned. This should be the goal. By doing this, you use your natural and unique talents, thoughts, and abilities to devise a masterpiece of an idea.

As an entrepreneur, I constantly challenge myself to read books, watch movies or videos, and listen to recordings on other entrepreneurs. I do this daily. As the thoughts that I generate from doing these things occur, I find myself eager to write the new idea or concept that I have in my mind down on paper. The next step I strive to do is to take action on that idea or concept by beginning the process of bringing it to life. If an obstacle occurs during the process, I seek out help, as well as educate myself about the problem that I'm having and why it has occurred. Overall, educating yourself can be a great benefit. Find out what way of learning works best for you. Then put all of your efforts into learning as much as you possibly can about your area of expertise using that learning style. Once you become consistent in your approach to learning, try other learning styles to maintain a high interest level.

Build a Team

When building a team, take your time to make sure that the people you bring on board with you are a good fit. Some of the attributes you want to look for are trustworthiness, honesty, level of commitment, loyalty, and good communication skills. These are not all of the qualities that you should look for in an individual, but they are important. You may be asking right now, who should I have on my team? Well, to start, hire a good lawyer and accountant. This is important and should be done. Finding a graphic designer, mobile app developer, as well as a marketing team (SEO, email, social media, print media), and an office assistant are other important team members to consider. If you want to take on a business partner, this person would be a part of your team as well. Consideration should be given to what you want to accomplish by adding a specific team member. Clearly be able to explain how adding that particular individual will help bring your product or service business to life.

When I started out on my very first business venture, I tried to do everything on my own. I was choosing to do this because at the time I didn't think that anyone would take my business idea serious. I thought to myself, a lawyer or accountant would probably ignore my calls or tell me that my idea was bad. In the end, I destroyed my own hopes of getting that particular business up and running because of my own thinking, lack of knowledge at the time, and actions. I learned from this experience.

Having a team that has your best interest in mind is important. They will help you along your journey. Don't use negative self-talk as a way out. If you can't assemble everyone that you need on your team all at once, start with the individual that you feel is the most important of all and will help get your product or service business into existence the quickest.

Be Persistent

An important factor in the success or failure of an idea is having the ability to bounce back positively to a defeat or after hearing someone say the word "No" to your idea. There are many pitfalls and hurdles that will have you feeling down and out. Being persistent in how you approach marketing and selling your product or service business is important. You have to sometimes clearly explain detail-by-detail to an individual what your thoughts and plans are. This is done in order for them to share the same vision about how you see your product or service benefiting the world. If they still don't see it, try again and again until they do. Let's say for example that you are discussing with a graphic designer how you would like your product package designed. The graphic designer quotes you an unreasonably high price. After several attempts of explaining your idea to them you begin to realize that he/she does not have the same vision that you have. Don't get discouraged; just reach out to other graphic designers until you find a person that fits into your budget for what you want designed. They also should be able to understand your vision.

Another strategic area to be persistent in is improving or developing some aspects or areas of your product or service business idea on a daily basis. There is nothing that should get in your way or distract you from developing your idea. Whether it's keeping an appointment with a mentor to making another call to a manufacturer, the development of a product or service depends on how persistent its leader or founder is. The amount of personal drive, determination, and commitment in the individual will play a major factor in the individual's ability to bounce back after a defeat or let down. If you are someone that needs more personal drive, find something that you love to do and have a sincere care about. Create a product or service business based on what you love to do. Your personal drive should increase because you have a motive to care.

There was a time when I was seeking out help to create and print a logo that I had sketched on paper. I wanted to use the logo on t-shirts. I first tried explaining it and showing the handwritten copy of the design to a printing company. At first they couldn't get the logo exactly how I wanted it. I was stuck with a choice. Should I go with what they have designed for me? Should I continue to explain in even more detail what I wanted? I chose the latter. It took several back and forth emails and phone calls, but it was worth it in the end. Persistence pays off!

Chapter 1

Chapter 1

Creating a Product from an Idea

The ideas that you generate from your mind has to come from what you are most passionate about. Knowing how everything will work does not matter as much as the concept of the idea you have in your mind. To begin the process of coming up with a product, start with an idea that improves a current product that you are passionate about. If there is a way to create an entirely new product that makes the world a better place then write down ideas based on that. Ask yourself, what can make a person happy and genuinely satisfied if they bought the product that I create? Ideas will begin to flow through your mind. Sort and find the right one, based on what you've written down. Put yourself in the shoes of a passionate customer. Whatever you feel the most confident about, and you are always thinking of, then that's the product to choose to create. Sometimes you may have a difficult time coming up with ideas. What follows are strategies to use when you can't think of any ideas for a product. They are idea mapping, past requests, proven passions, and future help. A description of each strategy follows.

Idea Mapping:

Idea mapping can be described as a kind of domino effect. You start by writing a word, concept, sport, or something that you are passionate about down in the middle of a blank sheet of paper. Put a box around it. Then draw a line away from it, and draw another box. Inside this box, you are to write down any idea, concept, service, or money generating business that helps people that you can think of. Be as creative as possible. Do this with no limitations. Draw as many lines and boxes as you can fit on the sheet of paper. Then fill them with ideas and concepts.

Past Requests:

When a person or group always recommend or ask you to speak, perform a service, or use a product that you have created; this is an idea or concept that should be developed and turned into a business. Whether you are good at preparing speeches or have created an app that increases a coaches scouting ability. Use what you already are good at to an advantage. Develop your natural talents and abilities further by learning from other experts in your field. People are going to you for a reason. Use this as a hint to explore your natural gift to the world.

Proven Passions:

Night and day you are thinking about it. When you talk to other people, it seems to come up during the conversation. The idea or concept that I'm describing is a passion for something that you have. It may have started when you were a little child or just gradually developed over time. Either way, the passion that you have for this particular sport, event, idea, concept, or way of life is very strong.

Future Help:

The world will be a better place in the future because this idea or concept was created. The more people it helps the more you are needed to bring the product or service business idea to life.

Other individuals may be needed to assist you in fulfilling your idea or concept.

Creating a product idea or concept is demanding and requires you to take action. Keep a notebook by your bedside. Write down anything that comes to your mind as you lay in bed at night or when you first wake up in the morning. The writing process is the second step to bringing your idea to life. Remember, the first step is the initial thought of the idea or concept. Next, action must be taken to begin to associate with people that can help you bring the idea or concept to life. This is done while protecting your idea or concept from being copied.

As a sports entrepreneur enjoy the brainstorming process. Take time to ponder and reflect on an idea or concept for an extended period of time. Analyze every detail. The vision that is seen should be of how it would look if it were fully developed and being used. Creating a sports product can be an exciting accomplishment for its founder. Pure love exists in the creation and care of the idea. The end product in most cases has been thought about for quite some time and it will show in the product quality. Embrace the entire process.

Sports Entrepreneur Tips #1

1. Think of ideas that would solve or help world causes. Create a packaged product based on helping others.
2. Find time every day to write ideas down on a blank sheet of paper. Keep a small pocket notebook.
3. Analyze all of your talents and abilities. Create a product using a talent or ability that you have. Think of a way to turn your talent or ability into a physically packaged product.
4. When someone says "It won't work" or "That's a bad idea", immediately think of two reasons why it will work. Say the two reasons to yourself repeatedly for one minute and then write them down in your pocket notebook or on a blank sheet of paper.
5. List all of your hobbies and the things you like to do in your free time. Think of a way to turn some aspect of your hobby into a packaged product. It can be a new product or you can improve an existing one.

Chapter 2

Chapter 2

Creating a Service Business from an Idea

Talents and natural abilities are unique to every individual. The awareness and understanding of how to maximize your natural talent and abilities must be accomplished. Some examples of natural talents and abilities are singing, speaking, teaching, training, massaging, technology, arts & crafts, building & design, coaching, etc. The talent and ability that you have should be nurtured. Identify other individuals who are experts in your area of talent and ability. Learn from them in any and every way that you can. By doing this you may be able to either form a partnership with the individual or develop a unique idea to improve the service business idea that you have in mind.

To become aware of a talent or what it is that you are naturally gifted at doing, reflect on what you do in your spare time. What did you do for fun as a child? What do you feel is easy for you, but others have a difficult time doing? The answers that you provide are the ideas that should be considered for a service business. Another way to find out what it is you are good at doing is shown through friends and the people who know you. Most of the time, your best friends or people that know you would say that you are very good at a specific thing. It may even be something that you do alone and are shy or afraid to do in front of others. These talents and abilities must be identified then acted upon. To act on them means to turn it into a service business that helps others. Again, clearly knowing what you are good at doing must be recognized first.

Sports service businesses range from personal trainers to massage therapy specialist. What follows are brief descriptions of seven sports service business areas that an individual can start. Use these descriptions as a guide to developing an idea for your own service business or branch off into a new and unique sports service business.

Personal Training Business:

There are many sub areas under this sports service business category. An individual who is knowledgeable in a specific area in a sport can provide training. Some areas include sport specific fundamental skill development training, strength & agility training, conditioning, life skills coach, sports psychologist, nutritionist, dietitian, or any other specialized focus area to help an athlete improve. Some areas that were mentioned require a certificate. Other areas may require an advanced degree. Whether you pursue the extra credential or not, you have to have clear and complete knowledge of your personal training area. The extent you are able to apply that knowledge and help others will determine your success. You will have to decide whether if you want to open your own office or facility to assist your clients or not. The other option would be to meet your clients at a local gym or another facility to provide services.

Gym or Fitness Center Business:

There may be products that go along with services in this business. Individuals of all ages strive to improve their health and way of life. The fitness center you design can be as creative as you imagine. Exercising and training are something that everyday individuals need to do more often. The natural talents and knowledge that you have gained as a business owner if nurtured, may benefit the health industry and help groups of people by the opening of this type of business.

Event or Recreation Facility Business:

There may be products that go along with services in this business. Creating a fun, healthy, and family oriented environment is the foundation of the services provided by this type of business.

Parents and children want an escape from the daily routine. Businesses can have as attractions pastimes such as bowling, movies, gaming, arcades, bumper car areas, and other fun attractions. The creativity when designing a facility is key. Knowledge of future trends will help sustain the success of the business. Having knowledge of future trends help you to develop alternative ideas if the need arises to change and adapt to popular industry or consumer trends.

Chef:

If there is one opportunity that's unique, it's being a chef. Your creativity is always on display based on the food that you prepare. Opportunities are abundant. You can be a personal chef to professional athletes or entertainers, open restaurants, or create any other unique idea for a business that you decide based on your talent and natural abilities as a chef.

Speaker, Singer, or Teacher:

The ability to captivate an audience and help others reach their goals is the nature of this type of business. It requires a lot of practice and preparation. There are many ways that you can educate yourself and craft your own unique style and delivery of presentations. Opportunities to be a motivational speaker, singer, or teacher are just a few ideas in this category of business. Find out what you are interested in most. Determine what skills and talents you have and, then improve them by watching and learning from others that are in your area of interest. The opportunities in this industry enable you to develop a service business idea based on what you like and are good at doing.

Attorney, Accountant, or Other Professional:

Preparation for a service business in this area requires a commitment to your educational endeavors and your idea. If you have a unique idea as an attorney, accountant, real estate agent, doctor, or other professional that will help others in sports or the world as a whole, then take action and bring it to life. Determine what you will specialize in and map out a plan of action to develop your service business idea.

<u>Sports Marketing Business:</u>

The ability to market to different segments of the population in unique and creative ways is an in demand opportunity. Educate yourself as well as take formal classes to improve your talents and abilities. Find out what area of marketing you are interested in the most and have a passion for. Then brainstorm ideas and develop your business around your area of interest.

Overall, talents and natural abilities must be nurtured and used to create business ideas. In this way, you are using a strength that you possess to help others. Opportunities exist throughout the sports industry for a variety of specialized and unique business ventures. Determine how to best maximize your abilities and to improve the talent that you possess. Then bring your service business idea to life.

Sports Entrepreneur Tips #2

1. Seek out and obtain training and certification in your area of expertise. This will improve your customers' trust in your service business.
2. Track your daily habits to identify areas within your service business that can be improved. Also, monitor your spending.
3. Make time management a top priority when creating a service business. Find out how many customers you can help in a day without rushing the service that you offer.

4. Analyze what your friends and family say that you are good at doing. Think of a service business based on what you are good at.
5. Know the exact type of customer that will be using your service. Create an image in your mind of the customer using the service that you offer.

Chapter 3

Chapter 3

Protecting Your Product or Service Business Idea

There are five key ways to protect your idea. They are keeping your idea to yourself until it's fully protected, registering a copyright, registering a trademark, registering a patent, or using a non-disclosure agreement when working with people that are helping to design your product or service. This chapter will explain each way to protect your idea. Knowing when to fully express your idea to another person or organization is important. Whether it's explaining a small detail of your plan or discussing a concept. You must be careful not to trigger a tell-all moment. If you do happen to tell your idea too soon, you open the door for someone to copy it and them possibly protecting the idea or concept from being duplicated before you do. What follows are descriptions of ways to protect your product or service business idea.

Keeping Your Idea to Yourself Until It's Fully Protected:

This may be the hardest thing to do. You're met with so much excitement and determination.

You will go through the experience of first being afraid to discuss your plan with anyone because of the fear of your idea being rejected. Don't worry this is normal. Once you pass that stage, the next is when you decide to tell someone close to you such as a spouse, sibling, or friend. What happens if they decide to tell someone else? To fully be prepared to discuss your idea or plan, take action first by bringing it to life. Let your actions do the talking for you. Once you have either registered a copyright, trademark, or patent for your idea or concept then you are free to discuss it. You now would have some form of certified protection saying that it's your original work. If you need to discuss your idea prior to getting it registered, have the person or organization sign a non-disclosure agreement that is drawn up for you by your legal team.

Non-Disclosure Agreement:

This agreement provides a layer of protection to you when you are discussing your plan to bring your idea to life with others who are helping you design and create the product or service business. The individual could for example be a graphic designer, freelance writer, virtual assistant, web designer, etc. The nondisclosure agreement also known as "NDA", stops the person from sharing your idea or concept with others for a proprietary gain. If you are passionate about your idea and want some form of protection when forming your team, the use of a non-disclosure agreement is a good resource to have.

Registering a Copyright:

If you have written a book or poem, recorded a song, or have an artwork that you've drawn, then a copyright is a good choice for your idea. The US Copyright Office website, www.copyright.gov should be visited to find out how to register your original work correctly. You can do this alone, or you can hire a professional such as an attorney to register your original work for you.

Registering a Trademark:

If you have a slogan that you've come up with or if you've created a logo for your business, then registering it for a trademark is a good choice. Visit the US Patent and Trademark Office website www.uspto.gov to find out how to register your original work correctly. You are also able to perform a search to find out if someone has trademarked your slogan or logo already.

Registering a Patent:

The creation of a unique product, beverage, device, or other creations that can't be copyright or trademark protected fall into this category. The idea that you develop and bring to life hasn't been seen or created before. The patent protects your idea. Visit the US Patent and Trademark Office website www.uspto.gov to find out how to register your original work correctly. You can do this alone, or you can hire a professional such as an attorney to register your original work correctly. There are three main types of patents: utility, design, and plant patents. The utility patent takes longer to receive, but will protect your idea better than a design patent. A design patent is quicker to register and cost less than a utility patent. Plant patents protect individuals who develop and grow new and unique plants. Plant patents are the least registered of the three.

Protecting your idea is an important step. Seek out assistance from an intellectual property attorney to properly do so. Once your idea is properly registered as your original work, you will be glad that you took the time and extra measures to accomplish that. You also move closer to bringing your idea completely to life.

Sports Entrepreneur Tips #3

1. Know your competitors' strengths and weaknesses. Find ways to explore opportunities in your own business to capitalize on your competitors' weaknesses.
2. When presenting or speaking at events, make sure that your product or idea is protected by copyright, trademark, or patent before discussing it.
3. Don't give out too much information during "elevator talks."
4. When your spouse or significant other does not support your idea, do not continue to talk about it or explain details to them. Remember, they are talking to their friends or someone else about the situation too.
5. Identify the market segment that likes your product and has the most potential to buy. Identify creative and unique marketing strategies to reach this group.

Chapter 4

Chapter 4

Finding Someone to Design Your Product

To start the development of your product idea, draw it out completely on a sheet of paper. You may be thinking to yourself, I'm not an artist and I can't draw that well. That doesn't matter. What matters is the vision of the product that you have in your mind. If you need to draw stick figures to bring it to life, then do it. Once you have something drawn on the sheet of paper, other ideas and concepts will come into your mind. Design and draw it however you think and feel it should be. Remember, this is your own unique idea. Another alternative to drawing your design on paper would be for you to gather all of the materials that you need to create the product idea that you have in your mind. Once you create the prototype using the materials that you gathered, take a picture of it. You can use the picture to explain to others. When they look at the picture, they can use it to further enhance the quality and design of your product idea. Remember, the materials and products that you initially create do not have to be perfect. Just create what you envision in your mind.

A 3D graphic designer, web developer, illustrator, or another similar professional can be hired to further develop the idea that you drew on paper or created using material and took a picture of. The communication between you and the professional must be clear and concise in order for your idea to be designed exactly the way that you envision it in your mind. After a prototype of your idea or concept is developed, make sure that your idea is properly protected. Then seek out manufacturers who can produce your product. You will have to decide on the quantity that you want produced and where you want your product stored.

Making a product takes patience and clear communication between you and the people that you have help design your idea. When you decide on a manufacturer to produce your product, you may be faced with the cost of buying your product in bulk. It may cost less to produce your product in a different country outside of the United States. However, you may encounter more communication barriers if the only language that you speak and understand is English. Decide what's best for you and your plans for the product idea that you have. If you plan to sell your product for profit, then buying large quantities of your product at a low cost would be beneficial to you. Determining the price that you sell your product for depends on a lot of factors. Start with doing a market survey. Find out what individuals have an interest in your product. Research and find out about similar products and how much they cost. Overall, getting your product developed, designed, protected, and manufactured is a huge process and a major step forward. Take time to congratulate yourself, but there's a lot more to be done. Don't stop here, keep going!

Sports Entrepreneur Tips #4

1. When starting out, use cost saving approaches to hire someone to design your product.
2. Freelance websites are an effective way to search and communicate with potential product design team members.
3. Attend networking events in your local community to meet potential product design team members.
4. Placing help wanted ads online, in newspapers, and in magazines are ways to find and hire a product designer. Determine which way best fits your goals.
5. Choose a partner that will help bring your idea to life. The person has to be an asset to the vision and creation of your business.

Chapter 5

Chapter 5

Designing Your Packaging Box

The design of your packaging box starts with you knowing the type of customer that will be purchasing your product. That is, clearly identify the ideal person who will use your product. Some questions that you will have to answer when doing this are: What age range does my product benefit and appeal to most? What styles or fashions are popular with that particular age group? Do I want to sell my product in retail stores only, online only, or both?

When designing your packaging box based on a particular age group, certain types of styles and colors will stand out. For example, if you are creating a packaging box for perfume for teen girls, colors that may be popular may be found by researching current fashions in your target market. A style that would go along with the color chosen would have to represent qualities and traits that teen girls think highly of and believe in. Certain ideas, designs, and images would reflect that particular style.

Deciding whether to sell your product online or in retail stores is a big decision. It determines how you will design your packaging box. If you choose to sell in retail stores, a completely designed packaging box must be created and properly labeled. On the other hand, if you choose to sell online only, you have more flexibility to either decide to use a plain brown box and ship the product directly to the customer or to completely design a packaging box. The design of a packaging box for retail stores involve working with a graphic designer and establishing a Universal Product Code label (UPC) barcode that identifies the product that you are selling. Any cautions, hazardous, or other harmful problems associated with your product must be listed on your your packaging box. The graphic designer can help you with the proper placement of these items. There are various websites that you can visit to purchase a UPC Barcode. Just type the phrase "UPC Barcode" in a search engine.

Knowing the height, width, and weight of your product will help with the communication you have with the designers of your packaging box. Once the design is finish, you will then have to find a manufacturer to print the packaging box for you. When printing , you will have the choice to print a large bulk order of the packaging boxes or a small quantity order. The design process for the packaging box involves open and clear communication between everyone on your team. Picture how you envision your product on a shelf inside a retail store or online. Use that image that you have in your mind as a guide to create the packaging box.

Sports Entrepreneur Tips #5

1. Know where the best place to sell your product. Selling online and in retail stores are both good options.
2. Be aware of any economic factors that can influence the success or failure of your business. For example, a loss of jobs or a manufacturer closing its business in a local community would have a negative effect on the start of a small business in that particular location.
3. Analyze the supply and demand for your product. Find out how others in your industry price their product or service. Then strategically set the price for your product or service.
4. Be aware of current trends, styles, and fads within your target market when designing your packaging box.
5. Clearly identify your customer base. Know everything about them.

Chapter 6

Chapter 6

Finding Supplies for Your Service Business

The success of your service business involves purchasing and maintaining the correct amount of supplies that are needed to operate your business. Create a list of every item that is needed to get your service business started and to perform the specific service that you will provide. The administrative supplies needed should be included as well. As an example, supplies needed to start a personal fitness training business are as follows:

Supplies Needed to Get Started:

Resistance Bands
Light Arm and Leg Weights
Yoga Mats
Medicine Ball
Client Specific T-Shirts, weights, and training aids
Promotional Water Bottles

Promotional Key Chains
Other Personal Fitness Training Supplies
Administrative Supplies Needed:
Post Cards and Stamps
Client Forms
Staples and Stapler
Pen and Pencils
Note Pads
Printer Paper
Copyrighted Material
Printer Ink
Gym/ Workout Space Rental Agreement Form

The list above does not include everything that you would need and should only be used as an example. Some supplies needed would vary based on the type of service business you start. A service business such as a massage therapy business for example would have cost for oils, candles, massage table, and other massage therapy associated items. The supply needs would be different for a sport specific skills training service business. Regardless of the type of service business you start, supplies normally can be bought in large bulk orders or in small quantities. Identify the location where you will offer the services. Find out what's already available to you. Based on what's available to you, create your list of supplies needed to purchase.

Whether you start a massage therapy business or a sports agility training business, keep an accurate and detailed client list with notes. Have a backup copy as well. Based on the list of clients you have, specific supply needs will be shown to help the various clients more than others. Find out what supplies you are using most. By doing this, you will not waste your money on purchasing supplies that you do not use that often.

Sports Entrepreneur Tips #6

1. Decide how often you want to purchase supplies for your service business. Buying in bulk saves money and provides you more time before you have to order again.
2. Consider creating custom name products based on the supplies you purchase.
3. Cost saving is an important factor when purchasing supplies.
4. Consider opening a supplies business based on your service business industry.
5. Monitor your banking information when purchasing supplies online for your service business.

Chapter 7

Chapter 7

Building Your Team

This chapter will outline the key members to add to your team when building a sports business. When you begin as a start up business, explain your overall objective for the business to each team member and the importance of their particular role in the success of the business venture. The number of people that are a part of your start-up team will vary. What follow is descriptions of seven key members that typically are a part of a start up business venture team:

Business Partner:

This individual could be a friend, relative, spouse, or network associate. If you have a partner or multiple partners, clearly write out each partners' ownership stake in the business and their roles and responsibilities. Every agreement should be put in writing. This is especially important if your partnership involves a best friend or family member. Have an attorney involved to be a neutral third party when using contracts or forms. A business partner could also be a person that just provides capital for your business venture.

Accountant:

The individual that you add to your team in this role will assist you with annual tax filings for your business and overall financial wellness for your business venture. It's important that you have frequent and open communication with your accountant. The support given by your accountant should have your company's best interest in mind. Conduct several interviews with different accountants to find a good fit for what you are looking for as it relates to business accounting services.

Attorney:

It's very important to have a lawyer on your team. In order to find the right attorney to add to your team, meet and interview several attorneys. There should be a common interest in your idea or concept that you are bringing to life. The attorney will be able to assist you in deciding on a business structure, draft contracts, protect your intellectual property, and provide other services that will assist you and your sports business idea. There must be open and honest communication by all parties. It's good to have more than one attorney to be a part of your team. The two or more attorneys that you add to your team would handle different areas within your business. They would share the same goal which is to help bring your idea or concept to life.

Graphic Designer:

The individual chosen to be a part of your team in this role helps bring your idea or concept to life by designing what you have created in your mind and have written down on paper or built. It could be basic stick people drawings that you have on paper. The graphic designer will enhance your idea based on the explanation you provide. You have to clearly explain what idea or concept you want created. Every detail must be examined in order for your idea or concept to be designed correctly. Take time to view the previous work done by the graphic designer. This will help you find the individual that has the right design style you are looking.

Website and Mobile App Developer:

In order to let the world know about your idea or concept, a website or mobile app must be created. You can have both created. A choice will have to be made on whether to create the website and mobile app on your own or add a professional to your team to do it for you. The person you add in this role must clearly understand your idea or concept. Technology is constantly changing, so have a complete understanding of what services are provided by the website or mobile app developer and how their services fit into your overall marketing plan.

Office Administrative Assistant:

There will be a lot of tasks that take up your time. In order to relieve stress and anxiety do try to do everything on your own. Hire and add an administrative assistant to your team. This individual could be a virtual assistant or can work in an office. It's up to you. Meet and interview several individuals before you decide on someone. Make sure that you have created a list of tasks that you would want the person to complete. For example, the list might include mailing out letters, answering phones, responding to emails, drafting letters, planning events, filing important documents, etc.

Marketing Team:

It's important to add several individuals or organizations to be a part of your marketing team.

The graphic designer, website and mobile app developer, and administrative assistant may have marketing roles. Decide what ways you plan to market and reach customers. Then based on the marketing plan you create, find individuals or other marketing businesses to help you reach your marketing goals. Some ways to market to customers include print ads, radio, TV, and social media.

When building your team keep your end goal in mind. Ask yourself, will this person help bring my idea to life? If you can answer yes without any hesitation, then you are adding the right individual or organization to your team.

Sports Entrepreneur Tips #7

1. Know the length of service you will need for the accountants and attorneys that you bring on your team.
2. Get a second opinion when deciding on important aspects of your business
3. Interview several accountants, attorneys, and other professionals before deciding who to add on your team.
4. Ask friends or family for referrals to professionals they know or have had a good experience with.
5. Conduct background checks on all team members.

Chapter 8

Chapter 8

Writing a Business Plan

Writing a business plan is a great leap forward. You have your idea fully developed. Now you are providing a complete and detailed roadmap of how you will run every aspect of a business that's centered around your sports product or service idea. Whether it's forecasting your annual sales or outlining a strategy to manufacture and distribute the product, your business plan should be all inclusive. If you don't know where to start when writing a business plan, you have several options. You can use information that you find online or somewhere else to try and create a business plan on your own. There are freelance businesses that offer business plan writing services. Larger companies may offer business plan writing services as well. Lastly, you can get assistance and mentoring while writing your business plan through a local or national small business support agency. Listed below are the advantages and disadvantages of each choice to writing a business plan.

Writing a Business Plan Without Assistance

Advantages:

- You are self educating yourself.
- You get to view various sample business plans.
- You hold yourself accountable for completion of the business plan.
- There is minimum to no cost.

Disadvantages:

- Lack of knowledge and experience in writing a business plan.
- You hold yourself accountable for completion of the business plan.
- Some of the sections of the business plan may be written wrong because of a misunderstanding of the requirements.

Hiring Someone Else to Write Your Business Plan:

Advantages:

- It saves time (The plan will be completed in a timely manner).
- The business plan will be written by a knowledgeable and experienced individual or organization.

Disadvantages:

- The cost may be high.
- The business plan that's written may be too generic (It doesn't reflect your true business goals).

- Your idea is exposed to others (Have them sign a NDA).

Writing a Business Plan With Assistance From an Agency

Advantages:

- You are self educating yourself.
- The business plan will be completed in a timely manner.
- You have assistance and guidance from a knowledgeable and experienced individual or organization.
- There is minimum or no cost.

Disadvantages:

- Your idea is exposed to others (Have them sign a NDA).
- You may have less control of how the business plan is structured and written.

The business plan that's created will assist you in obtaining funding for your business venture. Make sure you are knowledgeable and able to present every section of your plan in front of a group of people. Read through the completed plan several times and practice speaking alone and in front of groups. The roadmap for your business is set. Now take action.

Sports Entrepreneur Tips #8

1. Create a management team for your businesses.
2. Find the general sales forecast numbers for your business by analyzing what your competitors' annual sales are and examining industry standards. Factor in any circumstances that would cause a lack of sales for your product or service.
3. Your company's bio should be genuine. Discuss how the business started.
4. A good mission statement and objective does wonders for a presentation for a loan or grant.
5. Use your sales forecast as a guide to meet or exceed expectations.

Chapter 9

Chapter 9

Seek Business Assistance

Business assistance involves learning from mentors, getting advice from friends or other successful individuals, educating yourself in all areas of your business and life, and learning from failures. The guidelines and limitations that you develop for seeking business assistance will improve your overall knowledge as well as improve the chances of your idea being brought to life. Keep an open mind when learning from others. For example, the information that the person mentoring you provides could have nothing to do with your idea or what you want to do with your business venture, but hear the person out. Find the hidden message within the information or story that they are talking to you about. Don't be afraid to ask questions. The more questions you ask, the better the advice you will receive.

Educating yourself involves reading books like the book you are reading now, attending seminars, watching videos, researching your business industry, listening to audiobooks and reading books on self improvement, and making mistakes. Keep a pen and notebook by your bedside. This will be a good strategy to use to end your day. Reflect on what you've learned that particular day and write down anything that you think of that's positive. Ideas will flow through your mind as well. Write the ideas down too. When you make a mistake, don't worry and get down on yourself. Learn from what you did wrong. Ask yourself how can I create a better outcome given the same scenario next time? To uplift and motivate yourself to bounce back from a failure, try listening to music that you listened to as a child or teen. This will most of the time foster a happy experience or worry free time period that you had. It also gives you a way to not think about the failure with a negative conscience.

Business assistance can include more than what's been mentioned. Anything or any individual that provides an answer to a problem that you are having when trying to advance your idea or business venture is regarded as a form of business assistance. Remember to protect your idea when discussing key concepts with others.

Sports Entrepreneur Tips #9

1. Get things done before the deadline.
2. Ask advice from others who are in the same business assistance program as you.
3. Attend seminars and workshops at least once a month.
4. Overcome setbacks in your business by reading your goals daily and exercising.
5. In order to bring your business or idea to life, face all of your fears and challenges head on.

Chapter 10

Chapter 10

Finding Money to Fund Your Business

The task of finding enough money to fund your business needs are ongoing. Many obstacles may get in your way when it comes down to funding a business venture. For example, a person who is self funding their business from a savings or retirement account may be faced with issues such as a car breaking down, the basement flooding, or some other unexpected problem that calls for their attention and money. Be disciplined on the spending that's done for all of your business needs. The two main goals when deciding to spend on business needs should be to bring your idea to life and to market your business continuously to the world.

There are several options that are available to assist sports entrepreneurs in getting money for their business venture. There are advantages and disadvantages to each option. There may also be other unique and creative ways to fund your business venture. This book will focus on seven key strategies to fund a sports business venture for start up companies. They are:

1. Self Fund Your Business
2. Ask Friends, Family, or Network
3. Apply for a Personal or Business Loan
4. Pitch Investors
5. Apply for Grants or Enter Contests
6. Seek Out Private Lenders
7. Use a Second Job to Fund Your Business

<u>Self Fund Your Business:</u>

This strategy involves several different types of self funding options. The first option is to have cash on hand at any time to fund what you need to grow your idea or business. The cash can come from multiple sources such as cash readily available, a sudden win fall, or good fortune. The key point here is that it's readily available to use. The second option comes from a deliberate effort to save money monthly strictly for growing your idea or business. An example here would be for instance, a person that makes $1,600 monthly from working a job saves $400 each month to expand their idea or business. The third option within the self funding strategy is the use of money saved over the years in a retirement account that's taken out to fund the business. Let's say a person has amassed $30,000 in a 401k retirement account over ten years from working a job. They withdraw the money and use it to grow their business. The last option in the self funding strategy is the pay as you go method. The person spends on the business sporadically or only when there is money left over from normal living expenses. This last option of pay as you go causes the time to bring your idea or business to life a long drawn out process.

Self-funding is the starting point in any idea or business venture. The spending may be simply to purchase a notebook to write ideas in. Regardless of the option or multiple options that you choose to use within this strategy, know your long-term plan for your sport idea and business venture. This will help you to spend smarter when attempting to grow your idea or business.

Ask Friends, Family, or Network:

Talking to a Friend or family member about your idea or business venture takes courage and the ability to handle rejection. Stay thinking positive regardless of the outcome. When you ask a friend or family member for money to help bring your idea or business venture to life, make sure the individual has a clear understanding and answer to the following questions: How much money do they have to lend you?, How long will it take for them to get their money back?, and What extra benefit will they receive by lending you the money? Most of the time, if all three of the questions are answered and understood by the friend or family member, the meeting as well as the outcome will be positive.

To determine which friends or family members to ask about helping to fund your idea or business venture, start by writing a list of every friend and family member you can think of. Don't leave anyone out. Now, at this point, you may be thinking to yourself "I don't want any of my friends or family members involved with my idea or business venture." That's perfectly fine. Still continue to write down every friend and family member that you can think of. You don't have to ask them for the money. The friend or family member may, however, know someone that you don't know who has the money to give. After making your list, those on it who share a common interest in your idea and business venture; talk to them first. If they do not want to give money or support your idea or business venture, kindly say thank you and ask them if they know someone who shares the same interest and if you can get introduced to that person. This must be done in order to fully exhaust all opportunities with the friend or family member who shares a common interest in your idea or business venture. After meeting and talking with every friend and family member that shares the same interest as you, the next step would be to go back to your list and begin setting up meetings and discussing your plans with everyone else that you have listed. If you decide not to meet with them; just informally ask the friend or family member when they are in your presence for an introduction to a friend or acquaintance that they know who shares a common interest in your idea or business venture.

Networking to fund your idea or business venture involves the same process. To create a list of network associates, write down the places or events that you visit or attend on a daily or weekly basis. Think about who you talk to or know at the location or events you attend. Write their names down. If you don't know their names, the next time you visit the location introduce yourself and find out their name. After your list is made, the same process that you completed with the friends and family list should be completed on the network list.

Apply for a Personal or Business Loan:

Applying for a loan requires you to know what type of loan best fits your need. Having good credit is a benefit, but individuals with bad credit do have options as well. There are five categories of loans that will be discussed. There may be other options as the growth of entrepreneurship is creating the need for unique lending strategies and lending institutions. The five loan categories are:

1. Personal Loans
2. Traditional Business Bank Loans
3. Alternative Loans
4. Loans that are Part of a Non-Profit Program
5. Crowdfunding or Peer to Peer Loans

Personal Loans

These types of loans require an individual to apply using their own personal information and the loan does not have to involve the business venture. The loan can be secured by a personal asset such as a car, boat, or house. The money that a person receives can be used in any way the individual chooses. If the individual defaults and does not pay the loan as agreed in writing, the secured asset can be collected from the individual. An unsecured personal loan is a loan that does not require list an asset as part of the loan. An individual can simply fill out an application, sign his or her signature, get approved, and receive the loan money. Having good credit is a plus when applying for secured or unsecured personal loans. For the purpose of this book, bad credit is defined as any FICO score 600 and below. Various banks require different FICO scores. Please check to find out what FICO score is the normal minimum requirement for approval for a loan in your area. Personal loans can be offered by traditional banks as well as other lending organizations.

Traditional Business Bank Loans

The loans in this category require the business to be a part of the loan. Your personal information will be needed when you apply for the loan as well. There are different types of US Government loan programs that your business venture may qualify for. There are some requirements that every business must meet when applying for a government loan program. The bank where you apply for the government loan program will assist you and explain what is needed to meet all requirements.

The traditional bank also offers business loans that are not a part of a government program. The business loans offered have similar requirements that the government loan program requires. Whether deciding on a small business government loan or a loan offered by the bank, find out who makes the final decision to approve or deny the loan. The effort that you give in preparing your business venture to qualify for the loan will move you closer to realizing your dream. Stay determined.

Alternative Loans

Loans in this category meet the needs of businesses in various stages. Whether your business is a start-up or well established, business needs such as for working capital, marketing expenses, or for equipment, financing is available specifically for these purposes. When applying for alternative loans, the process and requirements to get it may be lesser than when applying for a traditional business bank loan. However, the interest rate on the loan that you are approved for may be higher. This is the case when small businesses apply for a merchant loan. When you are approved for this type of loan, the company where you got approved gathers your banking information and gets paid by deducting payments from your checking account at a set time. So when your business gets paid, so does the merchant loan company. Most of the time, to qualify for this type of loan, a small business must be making a minimum amount of money annually.

Another example of an alternative loan that's available for small businesses is that a business can get a loan for the development, production, and manufacturing of their product if they already have a minimum number of customers who have already paid for the product in advance. This is called "invoice financing" or "accounts receivable financing." Like the merchant loan, the company that's approving the loan may deduct repayments for the loan out of your checking account at a set time. Personal credit scores vary, based on the company. Normally, companies in this category have lower credit score requirements than that of a traditional bank.

Loans that are Part of a Non-Profit Program

When you are seeking business assistance through a non profit organization, there are loan programs available that your business can qualify for if you complete the non profit organizations' business start up assistance or business mentoring program. In most cases, the assistance that's provided by the non profit organization prepares your business to meet the requirements of the loan.

When deciding on using this option as a way to finance your business, find out how much the personal credit scores factor into the approval process for a business loan.

Crowdfunding or Peer to Peer Lending

There are various websites that offer small business loans through a pool of individual investors. You normally have to create a user profile for yourself and a profile for your business on the website. Once your profile is complete, just request the amount of money that you are seeking. Then individual investors who are members of the website will decide if they want to provide money to fund your business or not. Normally, the personal credit score, the amount of money requested, and the time length of the loan are factors that the individual investors use when deciding on whether to fund your business or not. If you decide to use this option as a funding method for your business venture, view and compare several different crowdfunding websites before making a decision.

Pitch an Investor:

This strategy involves preparing every aspect of your business and yourself for a meeting with someone who has money to give. Knowing your marketing plan, consumer base, sales projections, and exit strategy (how you plan on leaving the business) are important when presenting your business to an investor. Anyone who requires taking a percentage ownership of your company as stipulations for giving you money for your business is an investor. There are different names and titles associated with an investor, such as venture capitalist or angel investor.

When presenting your idea to investors, know your company. Practice speaking. Practice your presentation over and over again. There are several ways to seek out investors for your idea or business venture. Entering a small business contest, seeking business mentoring, networking with friends and associates, and searching online through social media are ways to find investors. The question that you must ultimately ask yourself is, if giving up a percentage of my company worth the amount of money and resources that I am receiving in return?

Apply for a Grant or Enter a Contest:

This book will focus on two ways to find and enter a contest for the sole purpose of winning start up capital. One way is to search online and in your region for start up business competitions in your area of business. The competition may require or list certain criteria for the businesses that enter the competition. The criteria could be something such as the contest being open to businesses that have been open for zero to two years. It could also be pitching only your idea and concept or pitching your business plan to a group. If the contest is found online, the majority of the time you have to submit your business plan online as well. The second way to enter a contest can be found through business mentoring and other business assistance programs that have competitions included as a part of their program. Make sure that you have your idea protected by copyright, trademark, or patent before deciding to enter into a contest.

If you decide to structure your business as a non profit organization there may be grants that your business qualify for. Seek out help from your attorney when deciding on the best form of business structure. Search online and in your region for grants. There are guidelines to follow when applying for grants. Guidelines are specific and could include specific uses for the money. An example would be as part of grant money received, an organization must offer their services to a certain social economic class of the population and a certain number of hours may be required to be spent offering the services to that particular group.

Seek out Private Lenders:

Private lenders are individuals who have money in a retirement account, any other type of account, or just have the money to lend. They are willing to give the money to you in the form of a loan that must be repaid. Finding these individuals could be done by talking to friends and family or by networking. Once you find a private lender, clearly present your idea or business venture to them. Don't leave out any details.

Use a Second Job to Fund Your Business Venture:

Determine what your current availability is after working your full time job, after attending school, or after other life events. Then find a job that you can work and the earnings from the job go directly to the funding of your idea or business venture. It's best to open a checking or savings account where the money that's earned goes directly into that account. Let's take for example; you decide to work a part-time job and earn $700 a month take home pay. You decide to save $400 of the earnings each month in a separate account. The $400 is to go directly towards the funding of your business in some type of way. If you do this for ten months, you have saved $4,000 to fund your idea or business venture. Strategic spending and goal setting with your remaining income must be done. Stay motivated to continue to save each month. There will be times that you are tempted to withdraw money from the savings account. Overcome the temptation and strive to bring your idea to life.

Sports Entrepreneur Tips #10

1. Use smart judgment when dealing with cash advance companies.
2. In order to fund your idea or business, save $400 each month from a side job.
3. When you are broke, continue to create.
4. Home lines of credit are a good source of capital for your business venture.
5. In order to find additional funding for your business, read books, blogs, and articles on start-up business financing.

www.ingramcontent.com/pod-product-compliance
Lightning Source LLC
Chambersburg PA
CBHW072106290426
44110CB00014B/1848